Leonardo da Vinci

BY LINDA CERNAK • ILLUSTRATED BY J.T. MORROW

Published by The Child's World®
1980 Lookout Drive • Mankato, MN 56003-1705
800-599-READ • www.childsworld.com

Acknowledgments
The Child's World®: Mary Berendes, Publishing Director
Red Line Editorial: Editorial direction and production
The Design Lab: Design

Photographs ©: Leonardo da Vinci, cover, 1, 5, 11, 12–13,
14, 19; Janaka Dharmasena/Shutterstock Images, 6, 15, 17;
Leonardo da Vinci/Bettmann/Corbis, 8; Summerfield Press/
Corbis, 10; PoodlesRock/Corbis, 16; The Gallery Collection/
Corbis, 21

ISBN 9781626873513
LCCN 2014930689

Printed in the United States of America
Mankato, MN
July, 2014
PA02223

ABOUT THE AUTHOR

Linda Cernak has more than 35 years of experience as a freelance writer and in-house editor of children's classroom readers and student textbooks. Since 1994, Cernak has published numerous children's books in the subject areas of social studies, science, and the arts. In her spare time, Cernak enjoys painting, drawing, and creating stained glass sculptures.

ABOUT THE ILLUSTRATOR

J.T. Morrow has worked as a freelance illustrator for more than 25 years and has won several awards. His work has appeared in advertisements, on packaging, in magazines, and in books. He lives near San Francisco, California, with his wife and daughter.

CONTENTS

CHAPTER 1

The Renaissance Man

The year was 1466. The city was Florence, Italy. It was a time of learning and change. This exciting time was the **Renaissance**. Artists, inventors, and scientists were busy in the city. Among them was a teenage boy. His name was Leonardo da Vinci. This boy would become one of the world's greatest artists.

As a boy, Leonardo was a gifted artist. He spent hours studying plants and animals. He made **sketches** of everything he saw. As he grew older, Leonardo studied and worked with famous artists. He traveled to other cities in Italy, such as Milan and Rome. He worked on many paintings.

THE RENAISSANCE

The word Renaissance *means* rebirth. *Most people agree that the Renaissance began in Florence in the 1300s. It was a time of great learning. People became more interested in science. Famous books were written. Artists experimented with new ways to create paintings and* **sculptures**. *Some of the greatest works of art were painted during this time.*

*Leonardo da Vinci became one of the most famous
artists of the Renaissance period.*

But Leonardo liked to put things off. Different interests distracted him. It often took years for him to finish a painting. He even left some unfinished. Leonardo only completed about 15 paintings in his lifetime!

Painting was only one of Leonardo's talents. He was a scientist who studied nature. He also studied the human body. His interest in the human body helped him express his ideas in his art. He was also a mathematician, a musician, and an inventor.

Leonardo wrote notes about his studies. Some notes included ideas for things no one had ever thought of before. He drew sketches of his **inventions**. One of these was a

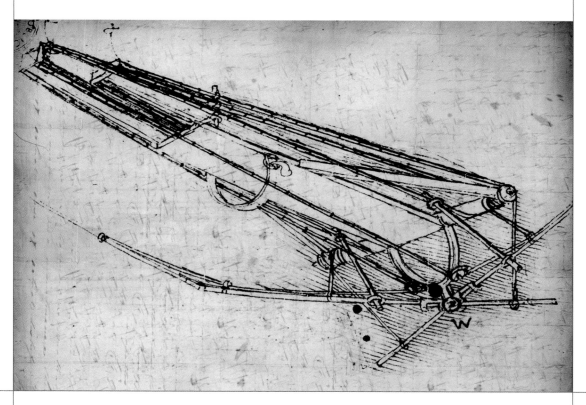

Leonardo sketched many different inventions, including a flying machine with wings.

flying machine. Leonardo kept these beautiful designs and drawings in his notebooks. Today, people can still see his notebooks, sketches, and paintings in museums.

CHAPTER 2

Becoming an Artist

Leonardo was born in 1452 in Vinci, Italy. His name means Leonardo of Vinci. As a boy, he was curious about everything. He studied nature and collected objects such as birds' eggs and animal bones. He then drew pictures of the things he collected. His father knew that Leonardo was a talented artist. So he sent him off to Florence, Italy. There, Leonardo began working for the famous painter Andrea del Verrocchio.

Leonardo studied all kinds of ways to create art. He drew sketches and made sculptures with clay. He learned to make paints by mixing

Leonardo studied and drew sketches of the many things he saw in nature.

colored **pigments**. Leonardo was one of the first artists to use oil paints. Oil paint dried very slowly. This way it could be painted in layers. Leonardo experimented with different brushstrokes using oil paints. As he grew, so did his talent.

PIGMENTS

Renaissance artists had to make their own paint. They did this by mixing pigments with egg yolks. A pigment is something that is added to a substance, such as dirt. The pigment gives the substance its color. Artists began to try new ways of mixing colors. Instead of using egg yolks, they began to paint with oils.

Most artists during the Renaissance painted stories from the Bible. Many showed pictures of angels and other holy figures. When da Vinci was about 20 years old, Andrea del Verrocchio let him paint an angel in one of his works. The angel was perfect. In fact, it was more beautiful than any of the figures Verrocchio had painted! Da Vinci was ready to be an artist on his own.

Soon da Vinci began another painting called *The Annunciation*. This painting also had an angel. The angel visits Mary, a figure from the Bible. The angel tells Mary that she will become the mother of Jesus. Da Vinci's studies of nature came in handy. His knowledge helped him paint the trees and mountains in the picture. He modeled the angel wings from his study of birds. Many people believe that this painting was da Vinci's first complete work. People still find it to be one of the most beautiful paintings ever.

Today The Annunciation *painting is in Florence. It is in a museum called the Uffizi Gallery.*

CHAPTER 3

Man of Masterpieces

When da Vinci was about 30 years old, he met the Duke of Milan. Da Vinci was already a famous painter. In Milan, da Vinci painted one of his most famous works: *Last Supper*. In this wall painting, Jesus sits at a table with his twelve **apostles**. The picture swirls with action. Light and shadows make the figures come alive. Each figure seems to be doing something.

No one had ever painted anything with such a special feeling of movement. *Last Supper* was a **masterpiece**. But the monks didn't think the painting was important. They decided to cut a doorway through the bottom of it.

FRESCOES

Many Renaissance artists painted works called **frescoes**. *A fresco is made by painting watercolors on wet plaster. The paint dries with the plaster, so it becomes part of the wall. Da Vinci decided to try a different way to paint a fresco. He painted on dry plaster and used different materials. His method didn't work as well. Last Supper began to flake apart soon after it was finished.*

It took da Vinci three years to finish Last Supper. You
can still see the painting in a church in Milan.

Da Vinci was one of the first artists to draw such detailed humans. He went to hospitals to study dead bodies. He even **dissected** them. He sketched hundreds of pictures of bones and muscles. He even made a sketch of a person's heart and organs. His sketches helped him understand the human body. This helped him express how the body moved. Other artists painted stiff, flat images of people. But the people in da Vinci's paintings looked lifelike.

Da Vinci also drew sketches to help him create sculptures. The Duke of Milan asked da Vinci to make a

statue. It would show the duke's father on a horse. So da Vinci started sketching. The statue was going to be the largest horse statue ever made. It would be more than 20 feet (6 m) tall! Da Vinci created the horse figure out of clay. Sadly, it was destroyed in 1499.

Da Vinci made dozens of horse sketches before starting his sculpture for the Duke of Milan.

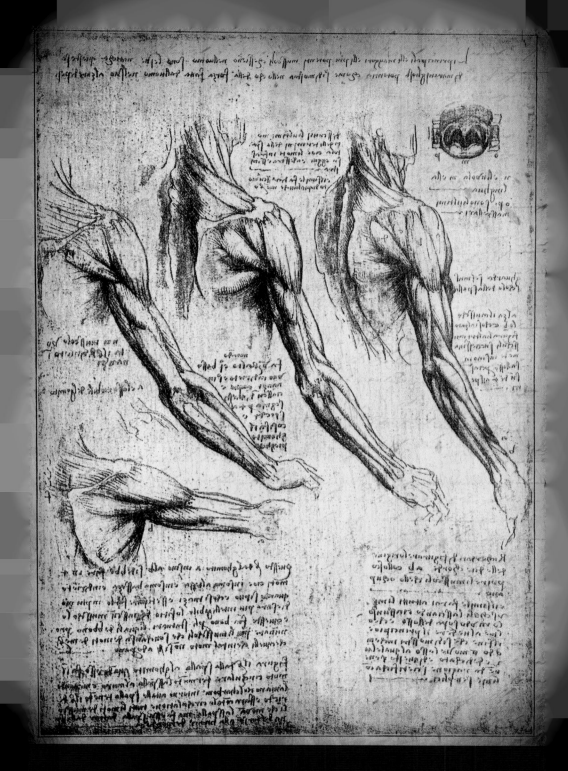

Da Vinci dissected, studied, and sketched human bodies to help him paint humans that looked as real as possible.

When da Vinci wasn't busy painting, sculpting, or studying nature, he was inventing. Da Vinci was bursting with new ideas. Many of his ideas were for things no one had ever thought about. His notebooks were filled with fantastic inventions. He drew sketches of waterwheels. He invented tools. He even designed a car. Da Vinci also thought a lot about flying. His studies of birds helped him design a flying machine.

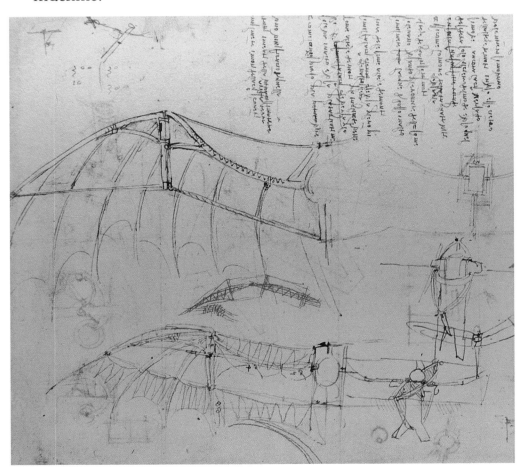

The wings of da Vinci's flying machine resembled giant bird wings.

The Duke of Milan was worried about armies attacking the city. So da Vinci invented machines that could be used to protect the city. He drew a giant bow that could shoot a giant arrow. One sketch showed a metal army car. As far as we know, none of his inventions were built during his time. But his ideas have inspired other inventors.

In this weapons sketch, da Vinci's invention of a giant bow is almost as tall as a human!

CHAPTER 4

Leonardo Lives On

When da Vinci was 51 years old, he went back to Florence. A merchant wanted da Vinci to paint a **portrait** of his wife. Da Vinci painted several portraits during his life. But none would become as famous as the *Mona Lisa*. Da Vinci painted the *Mona Lisa* with beautiful shadows and light. This made the painting incredibly lifelike.

Today the *Mona Lisa* is at the Louvre Museum in Paris. Millions of people come from all over the world. They want to see her famous smile. Some people wonder, "What is she thinking?"

Da Vinci only painted a couple more works after the *Mona Lisa*. But he was very popular for his paintings and inventions. Even Pope Leo X wanted da Vinci to paint for him. So da Vinci traveled to Rome. He stayed with Pope Leo. There, da Vinci started a painting. But he was often too busy doing other things. This drove the Pope crazy! Da Vinci only stayed in Rome for four years.

The Mona Lisa's *mysterious smile has fascinated viewers for hundreds of years. Her watchful eyes seem to follow you.*

During da Vinci's time, painters began using a new method. This method was called **chiaroscuro**. The word *chiaroscuro* comes from two Italian words. They mean light and dark. Da Vinci was talented at blending colors. Objects in light colors, such as people, seemed to pop out of paintings with a dark background. Da Vinci became known for painting with this method. He used it to paint *Virgin of the Rocks.* The light and dark shadows make the figures look real.

In 1516, King Francis I of France invited da Vinci to come live with him. Da Vinci spent his last years in France. The king loved to talk about ideas with da Vinci. The two of them became close friends. The king even gave da Vinci a house near one of his castles. There is a legend that the king held da Vinci in his arms when da Vinci died in 1519.

Artists all over the world have tried to copy da Vinci's paintings. People still study his masterpieces. His works of art have helped teach other artists how to paint. Inventors have learned from his notebooks. People have even built some of his designs. Leonardo da Vinci was truly a genius for all time!

CHIAROSCURO

Renaissance artists could blend colors easily. That is because they used oil paints instead of egg-based paints. Oil paints let artists paint with beautiful shades of light and dark. Da Vinci was one of the first artists to master this method.

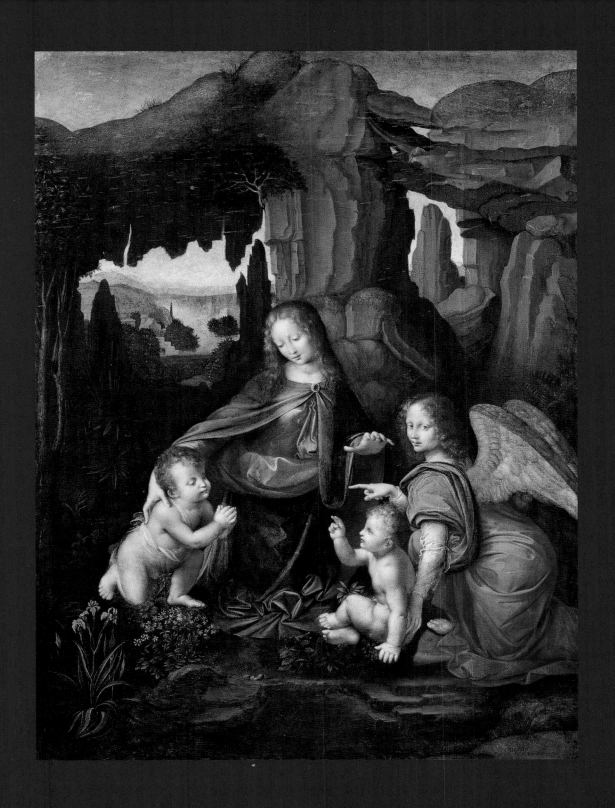

Da Vinci used chiaroscuro in Virgin of the Rocks *to light up the figures in the cave.*

Glossary

apostles (uh-PAH-suhls) Apostles are the twelve followers of Jesus. Da Vinci painted each apostle with Jesus in *Last Supper*.

chiaroscuro (KEE-ahr-uh-SKYOO-roh) Chiaroscuro is a method of using dark and light shadows in a painting. Chiaroscuro is used to help make paintings look more lifelike.

dissected (di-SEKT-ud) A human body or animal is dissected when it is cut apart so someone can study it. Da Vinci dissected human bodies to help him paint more realistic humans.

frescoes (FRES-kohz) Frescoes are paintings made on wet plaster. Many artists of the Renaissance experimented with fresco paintings.

inventions (in-VEN-shunz) Inventions are things that are designed or made for the first time. Da Vinci's invention of a flying machine was far ahead of its time.

masterpiece (MAS-tur-pees) A masterpiece is an artwork of great excellence. Da Vinci's *Last Supper* is a masterpiece.

pigments (PIG-munts) Pigments are substances that give color to paint. Da Vinci mixed a pigment with egg yolks to create his own paint.

portrait (POR-trit) A portrait is a picture of a person's face. Da Vinci's *Mona Lisa* is a famous portrait.

Renaissance (REN-uh-sans) The Renaissance was a period of great learning in the arts and science between the 1300s and 1600s. Da Vinci lived, painted, and created great works of art during the Renaissance.

sculptures (SKUHLP-churz) Sculptures are pieces of art carved and shaped out of stone, clay, wood, or other materials. Da Vinci created a horse sculpture out of clay for the Duke of Milan.

sketches (SKECH-ez) Sketches are rough or beginning drawings. Each sketch da Vinci made helped him paint or sculpt a final piece of work.

To Learn More

BOOKS

Brasch, Nicholas. *Leonardo da Vinci: The Greatest Inventor*.
New York: PowerKids Press, 2014.

Wood, Alex. *Leonardo da Vinci*. New York: Windmill Books, 2013.

WEB SITES

Visit our Web site for links about Leonardo da Vinci:
childsworld.com/links

Note to Parents, Teachers, and Librarians:
We routinely verify our Web links to make sure they are safe and
active sites. So encourage your readers to check them out!

Index